FISH & SEAFOOD COOKING

Designed by Sally Strugnell and Claire Leighton
Illustrations by Christine Berrington
Food photography by Peter Barry
Edited by Ros Cocks, Jillian Stewart and
    Laura Potts

CLB 3280
All rights reserved.
This 1993 edition published by Magna Books,
Magna Road, Wigston, Leicester LE18 4ZH.
© 1993 Colour Library Books Ltd., Godalming,
Surrey, England.
Printed and bound in Singapore.
ISBN 1 85422 590 1

FISH & SEAFOOD COOKING

MAGNA
BOOKS

INTRODUCTION

Versatility is one of the great attributes of fish cookery. It is not simply the fact that there are countless methods of cooking fish, but also it is a wonderful primary ingredient for any occasion ranging from a family lunch, in the form of a soup or quiche, through to a casual grilled supper dish. Fish is also perfect for an elaborate dinner party, whether it is simply grilled or served in a wine or cream sauce, while shellfish on the shell always look stunning and turn any meal into a special occasion.

It is to fish and seafood that the ever increasing number of conscientious objectors from the meat-eating world often turn. Fish is just as high in protein as meat, is lighter and easier to digest, and is also a good source of important vitamins and minerals. In recognition of this, and the growing popularity of fish and seafood, all big supermarkets now have fish counters, generally with a good selection of home and foreign produce with which to experiment. Where there is no fresh fish shop or counter, there is certainly always tinned fish, and this, too, can be used in a varied way and is excellent as a stand-by ingredient.

One of the drawbacks of buying fish and shellfish used to be the laborious and messy cleaning involved in their preparation. Not only is fish now more readily available, but it can also usually be cleaned and prepared at the counter. You can, for example, choose a piece of cod and have it cut into the number of steaks you require, whole fish will be gutted for you, scaled, trimmed, or whatever you require. Shellfish is often available practically ready to cook and can be bought on or off the shell. Cultivated mussels, for example, are a welcome change indeed to those of us who have slaved in the past with buckets and baths, trying to rid them of their numerous and stubborn attachments.

It is important to be able to tell good fresh fish and seafood from that which has been frozen and thawed and then kept hanging around. Fresh fish is always better in taste and texture, but where you do not have the choice, fish that has been frozen need not be passed over, as it may be the only opportunity of trying those varieties that come from more distant seas. A really fresh fish is slithery with a bright eye and black pupil, has firm elastic flesh and clean red gills. Shellfish should also look clean and bright. Cooked prawns and crabs should be brightly coloured as they fade with time and dry up. Lobsters and crabs should be heavy, and the tails and claws should still be springy, indicating that they were alive before being boiled. Shellfish, such as mussels and oysters, should be firmly closed if bought alive. Any open shells indicate that the creature is dead, and these must be discarded.

A freshly-caught fish is wonderful eaten with little or no adornment, such as fisherman's trout cooked over a campfire. However, in ordinary domestic circumstances it is fun to experiment with new and exciting flavours. White wine and cream are perhaps familiar to many as accompaniments to fish, but what about sherry and mustard, Tabasco and aniseed, or cumin and coriander, chilli and coconut? The possibilities for adapting fish and seafood are endless, and this inspiring collection of fish and seafood recipes reflects this by mixing traditional dishes with ones from all over the globe from Japan to France, Germany to Mexico, Spain to India, Italy to China.

Fish Tempura

Preparation Time: about 30 minutes **Cooking Time:** 2-3 minutes **Serves:** 4

This is a traditional Japanese dish, which can be served as an unusual fish starter.

Ingredients

12 uncooked large prawns
2 white fish fillets, skinned and cut
into 5 × 2cm/2 × ¾-inch strips
Small whole fish, e.g. smelt or
whitebait
2 squid, cleaned and cut into strips
2.5 × 7.5cm/1 × 3 inches long
2 tbsps plain flour for dusting

1 egg yolk
280ml/½ pint iced water
120g/4oz plain flour
Oil for frying
90ml/6 tbsps soy sauce
Juice and finely grated rind of 2 limes
60ml/4 tbsps dry sherry

Shell the prawns, leaving the tails intact. Wash the fish and the squid and pat dry. Dust them all with 2 tbsps flour.

Make a batter by beating together the egg yolk and water. Sieve in the 120g/4oz plain flour and mix in well with a table knife. Dip each piece of fish into the batter, shaking off any excess. Do not batter too many pieces of fish at a time. Only coat those you are able to cook.

In a wok or deep-fat fryer, heat the oil to 180°C/350°F. Lower in the fish pieces a few at a time and cook for 2-3 minutes. Lift them out carefully and drain on paper towels, keeping warm until required.

Mix together the soy sauce, lime juice, rind and sherry and serve as a dip with the cooked fish.

Crab and Sweetcorn Soup

Preparation Time: about 10 minutes **Cooking Time:** 8-10 minutes **Serves:** 4-6

Creamy sweetcorn and succulent crabmeat combine to make a velvety rich soup. Whisked egg whites add an interesting texture.

Ingredients

1 litre/1¾ pints chicken or fish stock
340g/12oz creamed sweetcorn
120g/4oz crabmeat
Salt and pepper
1 tsp light soy sauce

2 tbsps cornflour
3 tbsps water or stock
2 egg whites, whisked
4 spring onions for garnish

Bring the stock to the boil in a large pan. Add the sweetcorn, crabmeat, seasoning and soy sauce. Allow to simmer for 4-5 minutes.

Mix the cornflour with the water or stock and add a spoonful of the hot soup. Add the mixture to the soup and bring back to the boil. Cook until the soup thickens.

Whisk the egg whites until soft peaks form. Stir into the hot soup just before serving. Slice the onions thinly on the diagonal and scatter over the top to serve.

Szechuan Fish

Preparation Time: about 30 minutes (4 hours for the garnish) **Cooking Time:** about 10 minutes **Serves:** 6

The piquant spiciness of Szechuan pepper is quite different from that of black or white pepper. Beware, though, too much can numb the mouth temporarily!

Ingredients

6 chilli peppers for garnish
450g/1lb white fish fillets
Pinch salt and pepper
1 egg
75g/5 tbsps flour
90ml/6 tbsps white wine
Flour for dredging
Oil for deep frying
60g/4 tbsps cooked ham, cut in small dice
2.5cm/1-inch piece fresh ginger, finely diced
½-1 red or green chilli pepper, cored, seeded and finely diced

6 water chestnuts, finely diced
4 spring onions, finely chopped
3 tbsps light soy sauce
1 tsp cider vinegar or rice wine vinegar
½ tsp ground Szechuan pepper (optional)
280ml/½ pint light stock
1 tbsp cornflour
2 tbsps water
2 tsps sugar

To prepare the garnish, choose unblemished chilli peppers with the stems on. Using a small, sharp knife, cut the peppers in strips, starting from the pointed end. Cut down to within 1.25cm/½ inch of the stem end. Rinse out the seeds under cold running water and place the peppers in iced water. Leave to soak for at least 4 hours or overnight until they open up like flowers.

Cut the fish fillets into 5cm/2-inch pieces and season with salt and pepper. Beat the egg well and add flour and wine to make a batter. Dredge the fish lightly with flour and then dip into the batter. Mix the fish well. Heat a wok and when hot, add enough oil to deep-fry the fish. When the oil is hot, fry a few pieces of fish at a time, until golden brown. Drain and proceed until all the fish is cooked. Remove all but 1 tbsp of oil from the wok and add the ham, ginger, diced chilli pepper, water chestnuts and spring onions. Cook for about 1 minute and add the soy sauce and vinegar. If using Szechuan pepper, add at this point. Stir well and cook for a further 1 minute. Remove the vegetables from the pan and set them aside.

Add the stock to the wok and bring to the boil. Meanwhile, dissolve the cornflour in 2 tbsps of water. When the stock is boiling, add 1 spoonful to the cornflour mixture. Add the mixture back to the stock and reboil, stirring constantly until thickened. Stir in the sugar and return the fish and vegetables to the sauce. Heat through for 30 seconds and serve at once, garnished with the chilli pepper flowers.

Oysters Rockeffeller

Preparation Time: about 25 minutes **Cooking Time:** about 25 minutes
Serves: 4

Oysters can be purchased already opened, and you'll find the rest of this famous American dish simplicity itself to prepare.

Ingredients

24 oysters on the half shell
Rock salt
6 strips bacon, finely chopped
560g/1¼lbs fresh spinach, well washed, stems removed and leaves finely chopped
1 small bunch spring onions, finely chopped

2 cloves garlic, crushed
4-5 tbsps fine fresh breadcrumbs
Dash Tabasco
2 tbsps aniseed liqueur
Pinch salt
Parmesan cheese

Loosen the oysters from their shells using a sharp knife while holding them over a bowl in which to catch the liquid. Strain and reserve the liquid. Rinse the shells well and return an oyster to each one. Pour about 1 inch of rock salt into a baking pan. Place the oysters in the pan in their shells, pressing each shell gently into the salt.

Place the bacon in a large frying pan and cook slowly to render the fat. Turn up the heat and brown the bacon evenly. Add the spinach, spring onions and garlic and cook slowly until softened. Add the breadcrumbs, Tabasco, oyster liquid, liqueur, and a pinch of salt.

Spoon some of the mixture onto each oyster and sprinkle with Parmesan cheese. Place in a preheated 180°C/350°F/Gas Mark 4 oven for about 15 minutes. Alternatively, heat through in the oven for 10 minutes and place under a preheated grill to brown the cheese lightly. Serve immediately.

Fried Fish with Garlic Sauce

Preparation Time: about 30 minutes **Cooking Time:** about 3 minutes per batch of fish **Serves:** 4

Fish in such an attractive shape makes an excellent first course.

Ingredients

900g/2lbs fresh anchovies or
   whitebait
120g/4oz plain flour
60-90ml/4-6 tbsps cold water
Pinch salt
Oil for frying

Garlic Sauce
4 slices bread, crusts trimmed,
   soaked in water for 10 minutes

4 cloves garlic, peeled and roughly
   chopped
2 tbsps lemon juice
60-75ml/4-5 tbsps olive oil
1-2 tbsps water (optional)
Salt and pepper
2 tsps chopped fresh parsley
Lemon wedges for garnishing
   (optional)

Sift the flour into a deep bowl with a pinch of salt. Gradually stir in the water in the amount needed to make a very thick batter.

Heat enough oil for frying in a large, deep pan. A deep-sided sauté pan is ideal. Take 3 fish at a time and dip them into the batter together. Press their tails together firmly to make a fan shape. Lower them carefully into the oil, so as to preserve the shape. Fry in several batches until crisp and golden. Continue in the same way with all the remaining fish.

Meanwhile, squeeze out the bread and place in a food processor with the garlic and lemon juice. With the processor running, add the oil in a thin, steady stream. Add water if the mixture is too thick and dry. Add salt and pepper and stir in the parsley by hand. When all the fish are cooked, sprinkle lightly with salt and arrange on serving plates with some of the garlic sauce and lemon wedges, if desired.

Prawn Soup

Preparation Time: about 20 minutes **Cooking Time:** 8-10 minutes **Serves:** 6

This hearty fish soup makes a meal when accompanied by some crusty bread.

Ingredients

3 tbsps butter or margarine
1 onion, finely chopped
1 red pepper, seeded and finely chopped
2 stick celery, finely chopped
1 clove garlic, minced
Pinch dry mustard

2 tsps paprika
3 tbsps flour
1150ml/2 pints fish stock
1 sprig thyme and bay leaf
225g/8oz raw, peeled prawns
Salt and pepper
Sprinkling of chopped chives

Melt the butter or margarine and add the onion, pepper, celery and garlic. Cook gently to soften. Stir in the mustard, paprika and flour. Cook about 3 minutes over gentle heat, stirring occasionally.

Pour on the stock gradually, stirring or whisking until well blended. Add the thyme and bay leaf and bring to the boil. Reduce the heat and simmer about 5 minutes or until thickened, stirring occasionally.

Add the prawns and cook until pink and curled, about 5 minutes. Season with salt and pepper to taste and sprinkle with chopped chives before serving.

Moules Marinière

Preparation Time: about 30 minutes **Time:** about 15 minutes **Serves:** 4

Brittany and Normandy are famous for mussels and for cream and so the French combined the two in one perfect seafood dish.

Ingredients

1.5kg/3lbs mussels
Flour or cornmeal
430ml/¾ pint dry cider or white wine
4 shallots, finely chopped
1 clove garlic, crushed

1 bouquet garni
140ml/¼ pint double cream
3 tbsps butter, cut into small pieces
2 tbsps finely chopped parsley

Scrub the mussels well and remove the beards and any barnacles from the shells. Discard any mussels that have cracked shells and do not close when lightly tapped. Put the mussels into a basin full of cold water with a handful of flour or cornmeal and soak for at least 1 hour. During this time the mussels expel sand and take up the flour or cornmeal, which plumps them up. Meanwhile, chop the parsley very finely.

Bring the cider or wine to the boil in a large stock pot and add the shallots, garlic and bouquet garni. Add the mussels, cover the pan and cook for 5 minutes. Shake the pan or stir the mussels around frequently until the shells open. Lift out the mussels into a large soup tureen or individual serving bowls. Discard any mussels that have not opened.

Reduce the cooking liquid by about half and strain into another saucepan. Add the cream and bring to the boil to thicken slightly. Beat in the butter, a few pieces at a time. Adjust the seasoning, add the parsley and pour the sauce over the mussels to serve.

Coconut Fried Fish with Chillies

Preparation Time: about 30 minutes **Cooking Time:** about 30 minutes
Serves: 4

These deep-fried fishy bites are a real treat for lovers of spicy food.

Ingredients

Oil for deep frying
450g/1lb sole or plaice fillets,
   skinned, boned and cut into
   2.5cm/1-inch strips
Seasoned flour
1 egg, beaten
4 tbsps desiccated coconut

¼ tsp chilli powder
1 tsp ground coriander
½ tsp ground nutmeg
1 clove garlic, crushed
2 tbsps tomato purée
2 tbsps tomato chutney
2 tbsps dark soy sauce
2 tbsps lemon juice
2 tbsps water
1 tsp brown sugar
Salt and pepper

Sauce

1 tbsp vegetable oil
1 tsp grated fresh ginger
1 red chilli, seeded and finely
   chopped

In a frying pan, heat enough oil for deep frying to 190°C/375°F. Toss the fish strips in the seasoned flour and then dip them into the beaten egg. Roll them in the desiccated coconut and shake off the excess. Fry the fish, a few pieces at a time, in the hot oil and drain them on paper towels. Keep warm.

   Heat the 1 tbsp oil in a wok or frying pan and fry the ginger, red chilli, spices and garlic, for about 2 minutes. Add the remaining sauce ingredients and simmer for about 3 minutes. Serve the fish, with the sauce handed round separately.

Trout with Herbs

Preparation Time: 15-20 minutes **Cooking Time:** about 10 minutes per fish, plus 5 minutes to brown the butter **Serves:** 4

The miller (meunier) caught trout fresh from the mill stream and his wife used the flour which was on hand to dredge them with, or so the story goes.

Ingredients

4 even-sized trout, cleaned and
   trimmed
Flour
Salt and pepper
120g/4oz butter

Juice of 1 lemon
2 tbsps chopped fresh herbs such as
   parsley, chervil, tarragon, thyme or
   marjoram
Lemon wedges to garnish

Trim the trout tails to make them more pointed. Rinse the trout well. Dredge the trout with flour and shake off the excess. Season with salt and pepper. Heat half the butter in a very large sauté pan and, when foaming, place in the trout. It may be necessary to cook the trout in two batches to avoid overcrowding the pan. Cook over fairly high heat on both sides to brown evenly. Depending on size, the trout should take 5-8 minutes per side to cook. The dorsal fin will pull out easily when the trout are cooked. Remove the trout to a serving dish and keep them warm.

Wipe out the pan and add the remaining butter. Cook over moderate heat until beginning to brown, then add the lemon juice and herbs. When the lemon juice is added, the butter will bubble up and sizzle. Pour immediately over the fish and serve with lemon wedges.

Tomato Fish Stew

Preparation Time: about 30 minutes **Cooking Time:** 40 minutes **Serves:** 4

Cook any white fish you like in this tomato sauce. Serve with rice or potatoes.

Ingredients

Fishbones
1 bay leaf, 1 sprig thyme and 2
    parsley stalks
2 slices onion
1 lemon slice
6 black peppercorns
430ml/¾ pint water
90ml/6 tbsps oil
6tbsps flour

1 large green pepper, seeded and
    finely chopped
1 onion, finely chopped
1 stick celery, finely chopped
900g/2lbs canned tomatoes
2 tbsps tomato purée
Pinch salt and allspice
90ml/6 tbsps white wine
2 whole plaice, filleted and skinned
2 tbsps chopped parsley

Place fish bones, herbs, onion, lemon slice, peppercorns and water in a saucepan. Bring to the boil, then simmer 20 minutes and strain.

Heat the oil and add the flour. Cook slowly, stirring constantly, until golden brown. Add the green pepper, onion and celery, and cook until the flour is a rich dark brown and the vegetables have softened. Add stock and the canned tomatoes, tomato purée, salt and allspice. Bring to the boil and then simmer until thick. Add the wine.

Cut the fish into 5cm/2 inch pieces and add to the tomato mixture. Cook slowly for about 20 minutes, or until the fish is tender. Gently stir in the parsley, taking care that the fish does not break up. Adjust the seasoning and serve.

Baked Stuffed Mackerel

Preparation Time: about 15 minutes **Cooking Time:** about 30 minutes
Serves: 4

Mackerel should be eaten the day it is caught, so this is a recipe for people living near the sea.

Ingredients

60g/4 tbsps polyunsaturated
   margarine
1 small onion, finely chopped
1 tbsp medium oatmeal
4 tbsps fresh wholemeal
   breadcrumbs
1½ tsps chopped fresh lemon thyme

1½ tsps chopped fresh parsley
Freshly ground sea salt and black
   pepper
2-3 tbsps hot water, if required
4 mackerel, cleaned and washed
   thoroughly

In a large frying pan, melt the margarine. Fry the chopped onion in the margarine until it is soft, but not coloured. Add the oatmeal, breadcrumbs, herbs and seasoning to the fried onion, and mix well to form a firm stuffing, adding a little hot water to bind, if necessary. Fill the cavities of the fish with the stuffing and wrap each one separately in well-greased aluminium foil.

   Place each fish parcel in a roasting pan, or on a baking sheet, and cook in a preheated oven, 190°C/375°F/Gas Mark 5, for half an hour.

Chilled Fish Curry

Preparation Time: about 20 minutes **Cooking Time:** about 6 minutes
Serves: 4-8

This sophisticated, mild fish curry will serve four as a refreshing summer lunch, or eight as an elegant starter.

Ingredients
225g/8oz fresh salmon fillet
340g/12oz white fish fillet
Chicken stock
Salt and pepper
140ml/¼ pint mayonnaise
280ml/½ pint natural yogurt
2 tsps curry powder

Juice and grated rind of ½ lemon
120g/4oz peeled prawns

Garnish
Kiwi fruit, peeled and sliced
Sprigs fresh mint
Flaked coconut

Put the salmon and white fish fillets into a shallow pan and add just enough chicken stock to cover. Season to taste and simmer gently, until the fish is just tender. Remove the fish carefully from the cooking liquor and leave to cool slightly.

In a medium-sized bowl, mix together the mayonnaise and the yogurt. Blend in the curry powder and the lemon juice and rind. Flake the cooked fish, removing any bones and skin. Mix the flaked fish into the curry sauce, together with the prawns.

Arrange the fish curry on serving plates and garnish with slices of kiwi fruit, sprigs of fresh mint and coconut flakes.

Spicy Baked Prawns

Preparation Time: about 30 minutes **Cooking Time:** about 15 minutes
Serves: 2-4

This recipe is popular everywhere succulent prawns are available.

Ingredients

2 dozen raw large prawns, unpeeled
60g/4 tbsps butter or margarine
1 small red pepper, seeded and finely
    chopped
2 spring onions, finely chopped
½ tsp dry mustard
2 tsps dry sherry
1 tsp Worcester sauce

120g/4oz cooked crab meat
6 tbsps fresh breadcrumbs
1 tbsp chopped parsley
2 tbsps mayonnaise
Salt and pepper
1 small egg, beaten
Grated Parmesan cheese
Paprika

Remove all of the prawn shells except for the very tail ends. Remove the black
veins on the rounded sides, then cut the prawn down the length of the curved
side and press each one open.

Melt half the butter or margarine in a small pan and cook the pepper to
soften, about 3 minutes. Add the spring onions and cook a further 2 minutes.
Combine the pepper and spring onion with the mustard, sherry, Worcester
sauce, crab meat, breadcrumbs, parsley and mayonnaise. Add seasoning and
enough egg to bind together.

Spoon the stuffing onto the prawns and sprinkle with the Parmesan cheese
and paprika. Melt the remaining butter or margarine and drizzle over the
prawns. Bake in a pre-heated 180°C/350°F/Gas Mark 4 oven for about 10
minutes. Serve immediately.

Plaice and Mushroom Turnovers

Preparation Time: about 25 minutes **Cooking Time:** about 35 minutes
Serves: 4

These delicious individual fish pies make a warming lunch or supper dish.

Ingredients
4 plaice fillets, skinned
Salt and pepper
120ml/4 fl oz milk
120g/4oz button mushrooms,
  trimmed and thinly sliced
2 tbsps butter

Juice 1 lemon
3 tbsps hazelnut or lemon stuffing mix
340g/12oz puff pastry
Beaten egg for glazing
Poppy seeds for sprinkling

Season the plaice fillets and roll them up Swiss roll fashion. Secure each roll with a cocktail stick and poach gently in the milk for about 10 minutes in a preheated oven, 180°C/350°F/Gas Mark 4. Drain the fish and allow it to cool. Remove the cocktail sticks.

Increase the oven temperature to 200°C/400°F/Gas Mark 6. Put the mushrooms and butter into a pan with the lemon juice. Cook over a moderate heat for about 5 minutes. Allow the mushrooms to cool and then stir in the stuffing mix.

Roll out the pastry, quite thinly, into 4 circles, each 15cm/6 inches in diameter. Brush the edges with beaten egg. Put a fish roll into the centre of each pastry circle and top with a quarter of the mushroom mixture. Pull the pastry edges up and over the fish and pinch together to seal. Place the turnovers on a greased baking sheet and glaze with the beaten egg. Sprinkle with a few poppy seeds. Bake in the reset oven for about 25 minutes, or until well risen, puffed and golden. Serve piping hot.

Dressed Crab Salad

Preparation Time: 30-40 minutes **Serves:** 4

The rosy hued dressing used in this recipe is both creamy and piquant, the perfect foil for crab meat.

Ingredients

2 large cooked crabs
1 head iceberg lettuce
4 large tomatoes
4 hard-boiled eggs
280ml/½ pint prepared mayonnaise
60ml/4 tbsps whipping cream
60ml/4 tbsps chilli sauce or tomato
   chutney

½ green pepper, seeded and finely
   diced
3 spring onions, finely chopped
Salt and pepper
16 black olives

To prepare the crabs, break off the claws and set them aside. Turn the crabs over and press up with thumbs to separate the body from the shell of each. Cut the body into quarters and use a skewer to pick out the white meat. Discard the stomach sac and the lungs (dead-man's fingers). Scrape out the brown meat from the shell to use, if desired. Crack the large claws and legs and remove the meat. Break into shreds, discarding any shell or cartilage. Combine all the meat and set it aside.

Shred the lettuce finely, quarter the tomatoes and chop the eggs. Combine the mayonnaise, cream, chilli sauce or chutney, green pepper and spring onions, season to taste and mix well. Arrange the shredded lettuce on serving plates and divide the crab meat evenly.

Spoon some of the dressing over each serving of crab and sprinkle with the chopped egg. Garnish each serving with tomato wedges and olives and serve the remaining dressing separately.

Stuffed Sole

Preparation Time: about 30 minutes **Cooking Time:** 20-30 minutes **Serves:** 6

This North German sole dish is elegant enough for a formal dinner party.

Ingredients

60g/4 tbsps butter or margarine
2 tbsps flour
430ml/¾ pint fish or vegetable stock
90g/3oz button mushrooms, sliced
60ml/4 tbsps double cream
2 tbsps brandy
180g/6oz peeled, cooked prawns

120g/4oz canned, frozen or fresh
   cooked crabmeat
2 tbsps fresh breadcrumbs
Salt and pepper
6-12 sole fillets, depending upon size
60g/4 tbsps melted butter

Preheat the oven to 180°C/350°F/Gas Mark 4. Melt the butter and add the flour. Cook for about 3 minutes over gentle heat or until pale straw coloured. Add the stock and bring to the boil. Add the mushrooms and allow to cook until the sauce thickens. Add the cream and re-boil the sauce. Remove the sauce from the heat and add the brandy, prawns, crab and breadcrumbs. Season to taste.

   Skin the sole fillets and spread the filling on the side that was skinned. Roll up and arrange in a buttered baking dish. Spoon melted butter over the top and cook in the pre-heated over for 20-30 minutes, until the fish is just firm.

Smoked Haddock and Egg Quiche

Preparation Time: about 25 minutes **Cooking Time:** about 40 minutes
Serves: 6

This classic fish quiche is a firm favourite for lunches, buffets and suppers alike.

Ingredients
225g/8oz wholemeal dough
340g/12oz smoked haddock fillet
140ml/¼ pint chicken stock
2 hard-boiled eggs, chopped
1 tbsp chopped fresh chives

90g/3oz cheese, grated
3 eggs
280ml/½ pint milk
Salt and pepper

Roll out the dough to fit a deep, 22.5cm/9-inch fluted pie pan. Press the edges up well and push the base well down. Prick the base with a fork and bake blind for 15 minutes in a preheated oven, 190°C/375°F/Gas Mark 5.

Poach the fish gently in the chicken stock for about 8 minutes, or until just tender. Drain the fish and flake it into a bowl, discarding any skin or bones. Mix the chopped eggs, chives and cheese into the fish, and spread this mixture evenly into the part-baked dough case. Beat together the eggs and milk and season to taste. Pour over the fish mixture in the dough case. Bake for 25-30 minutes, or until the filling is set, at the same oven temperature as before.

Monkfish and Pepper Kebabs with Bearnaise Butter Sauce

Preparation Time: 30 minutes **Cooking Time:** about 25 minutes **Serves:** 4

Monkfish is a firm, succulent white fish, ideal for kebabs.

Ingredients

8 strips bacon, boned and rind
    removed
2 pieces lemon grass
900g/2lbs monkfish, cut into
    5cm/2-inch pieces
1 green pepper, seeded and cut into
    5cm/2-inch pieces
1 red pepper, seeded and cut into
    5cm/2-inch pieces
12 button mushrooms, washed and
    trimmed

8 bay leaves
Oil for brushing
120ml/4fl oz dry white wine
60ml/4 tbsps tarragon vinegar
2 shallots, finely chopped
1 tbsp chopped fresh tarragon
1 tbsp chopped fresh chervil or
    parsley
225g/8oz butter, melted
Salt and pepper

Cut the bacon in half lengthways and then in half across. Peel the lemon grass and use only the core. Cut this into small shreds. Place a piece of fish on each strip of bacon and top with a shred of lemon grass. Roll up the bacon around the fish. Thread each fish and bacon roll onto kebab skewers, alternating with the pepper, mushrooms and bay leaves. Brush well with oil. Cook under a moderate grill for 15 minutes, turning frequently and brushing with more oil, if necessary, until the fish is cooked.

Heat together the wine, vinegar and shallots in a small saucepan until they are boiling. Cook rapidly until reduced by half. Stir in the herbs and lower the heat. Beat in the butter, a little at a time, until the sauce is the thickness of a Hollandaise. Season to taste and serve with the kebabs.

Paella

Preparation Time: 30-40 minutes **Cooking Time:** 35-40 minutes **Serves:** 6

This dish has as many variations as Spain has cooks! Fish, seafood and poultry combine with vegetables and rice to make a complete meal.

Ingredients

12 mussels in their shells
6 clams (if not available use 6 more mussels)
12 Mediterranean prawns
3 chorizos or other spicy sausages
900g/2lbs chicken cut in 12 serving-size pieces
1 small onion, chopped
1 clove garlic, crushed
2 small peppers, red and green, seeded and shredded

450g/1lb long grain rice
Large pinch saffron
1150ml/2 pints boiling water
Salt and pepper
180g/6oz cod, skinned and cut into 5cm/2 inch pieces
120g/4oz frozen peas
3 tomatoes, peeled, seeded and chopped or shredded

Scrub the mussels and clams well to remove beards and barnacles. Discard any with broken shells or those that do not close when tapped. Leave the mussels and clams to soak in water with a handful of flour for at least an hour. This cleans them of sand and plumps them up. Remove the heads and legs from the prawns, if desired, but leave on the tail shells.

Place the sausages in a saucepan and cover with water. Bring to the boil and then simmer for 5 minutes. Drain and slice into 5mm/¼ inch rounds. Set aside.

Heat the oil and fry the chicken pieces, browning evenly on both sides. Remove and drain on paper towels. Add the sausage, onions, garlic and peppers to the oil in the frying pan and fry briskly for about 3 minutes. Combine the sausage mixture with uncooked rice and saffron and place in a special Paella dish or a large oven- and flame-proof casserole. Pour on the water, season with salt and pepper and bring to the boil. Stir occasionally and allow to boil for about 2 minutes. Add the chicken pieces and place in a preheated 200°C/400°F/Gas Mark 6 oven for about 15 minutes.

Add the clams, mussels, prawns, cod and peas and cook a further 10-15 minutes or until the rice is tender, chicken is cooked and mussels and clams open. Discard any that do not open. Add the tomatoes 5 minutes before the end of cooking time and serve immediately.

Fish Milanese

Preparation Time: 1 hour **Cooking Time:** about 6 minutes **Serves:** 4

These fish, cooked in the style of Milan, have a crispy crumb coating and the fresh tang of lemon juice.

Ingredients

8 sole or plaice fillets
2 tbsps dry vermouth
90ml/6 tbsps olive oil
1 bay leaf
Salt and pepper
Seasoned flour for dredging
2 eggs, lightly beaten
Dry breadcrumbs
Oil for shallow frying

90g/6 tbsps butter
1 clove garlic, crushed
2 tsps chopped parsley
1 tsp chopped fresh oregano
2 tbsps capers
Juice of 1 lemon
Salt and pepper
Lemon wedges and parsley to
  garnish

Skin the fillets with a sharp filleting knife. Remove any small bones and place the fillets in a large, shallow dish. Combine the vermouth, oil and bay leaf in a small saucepan, season to taste, and heat gently. Allow to cool completely and pour over the fish. Leave the fish to marinate for about 1 hour, turning them occasionally.

Remove the fish from the marinade and dredge lightly with the seasoned flour. Dip the fillets into the beaten egg to coat, or use a pastry brush to brush the egg onto the fillets. Dip the egg-coated fillet into the breadcrumbs, pressing the crumbs on firmly. Heat the oil in a large frying pan. Add the fillets and cook slowly on both sides until golden brown. Cook for about 3 minutes on each side, remove and drain on paper towels.

Pour the oil out of the frying pan and wipe it clean. Add the butter and the garlic and cook until both turn a light brown. Add the herbs, capers and lemon juice, season to taste and pour immediately over the fish. Garnish with lemon wedges and sprigs of parsley.

Salmon Pies

Preparation Time: about 30 minutes **Cooking Time:** about 35 minutes
Serves: 4

Canned pink salmon is used here in a very unusual and tasty way.

Ingredients

Pastry
225g/8oz plain flour, sifted
Pinch salt
120-180g/4-6oz butter or margarine
Cold water

Filling
1 large can pink salmon

3 tbsps oil
3 tbsps flour
½ green pepper, seeded and finely
   diced
2 spring onions, finely chopped
1 stick celery, finely chopped
280ml/½ pint milk
Salt and pepper

Sift the flour in a bowl with a pinch of salt and rub in the butter or margarine until the mixture resembles breadcrumbs. Add enough cold water to bring the mixture together. Knead into a ball, wrap well and chill for about 30 minutes before use.

Drain salmon and remove any skin. Discard small bones. Heat the oil in a small saucepan for the filling and add the flour. Cook slowly, stirring constantly until the flour turns a rich dark brown. Add the remaining filling ingredients except the salmon, stirring constantly while adding the milk. Bring to the boil, reduce the heat and cook for about 5 minutes. Add the salmon to the sauce.

Divide the pastry into 4 and roll out each portion on a lightly-floured surface to about 5mm/¼ inch thick. Line individual flan or pie dishes with the pastry, pushing it carefully onto the base and down the sides, taking care not to stretch it. Trim off excess pastry and reserve. Place a sheet of greaseproof paper or foil on the pastry and pour on rice, pasta or baking beans to come halfway up the sides. Bake the pastry blind for about 10 minutes in a pre-heated 200°C/400°F/ Gas Mark 6 oven. Remove the paper and beans and bake for an additional 5 minutes to cook the base.

Spoon in the filling and roll out any pastry trimmings to make a lattice pattern on top. Bake a further 10 minutes to brown the lattice and heat the filling. Cool slightly before serving.

Grilled Herrings with Dill and Mustard

Preparation Time: about 10 minutes **Cooking Time:** 12-15 minutes **Serves:** 4

Dill and mustard give herring a delicious tangy flavour.

Ingredients
4 tbsps chopped fresh dill
6 tbsps mild Swedish mustard
2 tbsps lemon juice or white wine
4-8 fresh herrings, cleaned but heads
   and tails left on

2 tbsps butter or margarine, melted
Salt and pepper

Mix the dill, mustard and lemon juice or wine together thoroughly. Cut three slits, just piercing the skin, on both sides of each herring and lay them on a grill pan. Spread half the mustard mixture equally over the exposed side of each fish, pushing some into the cuts. Spoon a little of the melted butter over each herring, and grill the fish for 5-6 minutes.

Turn the fish over and spread the remaining mustard and dill mixture over them. Spoon over the remaining melted butter and grill for a further 5-6 minutes. Sprinkle the fish with a little salt and pepper before serving.

Fisherman's Stew

Preparation Time: about 20 minutes **Cooking Time:** about 45 minutes
Serves: 4-6

This quick, economical and satisfying fish dish will please any fish lover for lunch or a light supper.

Ingredients

90ml/6 tbsps olive oil
2 large onions, sliced
1 red pepper, seeded and sliced
120g/4oz mushrooms, sliced
450g/1lb canned tomatoes
Pinch dried thyme

Pinch salt and pepper
430ml/¾ pint water
900/2lbs white fish fillets, skinned
140ml/¼ pint white wine
2 tbsps chopped parsley

Heat the oil in a large saucepan and add the onions. Cook until beginning to look translucent. Add the pepper and cook until the vegetables are softened. Add the mushrooms and the tomatoes and bring the mixture to the boil. Add thyme, salt, pepper and water and simmer for about 30 minutes.

Add the fish and wine and cook until the fish flakes easily, about 15 minutes. Stir in parsley.

To serve, place a piece of toasted French bread in the bottom of the soup bowl and spoon over the fish stew.

Spiced Salmon Steaks

Preparation Time: 15 minutes, plus 1 hour standing time **Cooking Time:** 12-15 minutes **Serves:** 4

A blend of spices and sugar makes this easy-to-prepare salmon dish very out of the ordinary.

Ingredients

120g/4oz light brown sugar
1 tbsp ground allspice
1 tbsp mustard powder
1 tbsp grated fresh ginger
4 salmon steaks, 2.5cm/1 inch thick
1 cucumber

1 bunch spring onions
2 tbsps butter
1 tbsp lemon juice
2 tsps chopped fresh dill weed
1 tbsp chopped fresh parsley
Salt and pepper

Mix the sugar and spices together and rub the mixture into the surface of both sides of the salmon steaks. Allow the salmon steaks to stand for at least 1 hour in the refrigerator.

Meanwhile prepare the vegetables. Peel the cucumber and cut into quarters lengthways. Remove the seeds and cut each quarter into 2.5cm/1-inch pieces. Trim the roots from the spring onions and cut down some, but not all, of the green part. Put the cucumber and spring onions into a saucepan, along with the butter, lemon juice, dill, parsley and seasoning. Cook over a moderate heat for about 10 minutes, or until the cucumber is tender and turning translucent.

Put the salmon steaks under a preheated moderate grill and cook for about 5-6 minutes on each side. Serve with the cucumber and spring onion accompaniment.

Sardine and Tomato Gratinée

Preparation Time: 20-25 minutes **Cooking Time:** about 15 minutes **Serves:** 4

Fresh sardines are becoming more widely available and this recipe makes the most of these delicious fish.

Ingredients
3 tbsps olive oil
900g/2lbs large fresh sardines, descaled and cleaned
2 leeks, cleaned and sliced
140ml/¼ pint dry white wine
225g/8oz tomatoes, skinned and quartered

Salt and pepper
2 tbsps each chopped fresh basil and parsley
4 tbsps Parmesan cheese, grated
4 tbsps dry breadcrumbs

Heat the oil in a frying pan and fry the sardines, until they are brown on both sides. It may be necessary to do this in several batches, to prevent the fish from breaking up. When all the sardines are cooked, set them aside and cook the leeks gently in the sardine oil. When the leeks are soft, pour in the wine and boil rapidly, until it is reduced by about two thirds. Add the tomatoes, seasoning and herbs to the leeks and cook for about 1 minute.

Pour the vegetables into an ovenproof dish and lay the sardines on top. Sprinkle the cheese and breadcrumbs evenly over the sardines and bake in a preheated oven, 225°C/425°F/Gas Mark 7, for about 5 minutes.

Halibut and Crab Hollandaise

Preparation Time: about 15 minutes **Cooking Time:** about 20 minutes
Serves: 4

Rich and creamy, the Hollandaise sauce adds an air of sophistication to this lovely fish and seafood dish.

Ingredients

4 large fillets of halibut
1 bay leaf
Slice of onion
75ml/5 tbsps white wine
1 tbsp butter
2 tbsps flour
2 tbsps double cream
Salt and pepper

225g/8oz crab meat

Hollandaise Sauce
2 egg yolks
1 tbsp lemon juice
Pinch cayenne pepper
Pinch paprika pepper
120g/4oz butter, melted

Put the fish with the bay leaf, onion slice, wine and just enough water to cover the fish, into a baking dish. Cover and cook in a preheated oven, 160°C/325°F/ Gas Mark 3, for 10 minutes.

Put the egg yolks, lemon juice, cayenne and paprika into a liquidizer, or food processor. Turn the machine on and gradually pour in the melted butter. Continue processing, until the Hollandaise sauce is thick. Set aside.

Put the 1 tbsp unmelted butter into a saucepan, melt over a gentle heat and stir in the flour. Cook gently for 1 minute. Remove the fish from the baking dish and strain the cooking liquor onto the flour and butter in the saucepan, stirring well, to prevent lumps from forming. Cook this sauce gently, until it is smooth and has thickened. Stir in the cream, but do not allow to boil. Season to taste. Stir the crab meat into the fish stock sauce and pour this mixture into a flameproof dish. Lay the halibut fillets on top and cover these with the Hollandaise sauce. Brown under a hot grill before serving.

Cod Curry

Preparation Time: about 15 minutes   **Cooking Time:** about 20 minutes
Serves: 4

The fragrant spices used in this fish recipe are now available at most supermarkets.

Ingredients

1 large onion, chopped
3 tbsps vegetable oil
2.5cm/1-inch piece cinnamon stick
1 bay leaf
1 tsp ginger paste
1 tsp garlic paste
1 tsp chilli powder
1 tsp ground cumin
1 tsp ground coriander

¼ tsp ground turmeric
140ml/¼ pint natural yogurt or
   225g/8oz can tomatoes, chopped
1-2 fresh green chillies, chopped
2 sprigs fresh coriander leaves,
   chopped
1lb cod cutlets, or fillets, cut into
   5cm/2-inch pieces
1 tsp salt

In a large heavy-based saucepan, fry the onion in the oil until golden brown. Add the cinnamon, bay leaf and the ginger and garlic pastes and fry for 1 minute. Add the ground spices and fry for a further minute, then stir in *either* the yogurt or the canned tomatoes, and add the chopped chillies and coriander leaves.

Only if you have used yogurt, stir in 140ml/¼ pint water and simmer the mixture for 2-3 minutes. Do not add any water if you have used the canned tomatoes.

Stir the cod into the sauce, and add the salt. Cover the pan and simmer for 15-18 minutes before serving.

Mussels in White Wine Sauce

Preparation Time: about 30 minutes **Cooking Time:** 5-8 minutes **Serves:** 4

Mussels in season are very economical. Most fishmongers sell them and so do supermarkets that have fresh fish counters.

Ingredients
2kg/4½lbs mussels in their shells
Flour or cornmeal
280ml/½ pint dry white wine
1 large onion, finely chopped
2-4 cloves garlic, finely chopped

Salt and coarsely ground black
  pepper
2 bay leaves
225g/8oz butter, melted
Juice of 1 lemon

Scrub the mussels well and remove any barnacles and beards (seaweed strands). Use a stiff brush to scrub the shells, and discard any mussels with broken shells or those that do not close when tapped. Place the mussels in a basin full of cold water with a handful of flour and leave to soak for at least an hour. During this time the mussels expel sand and take up the flour or cornmeal, which plumps them up.

Drain the mussels and place them in a large, deep saucepan with the remaining ingredients, except the butter and lemon juice. Cover the pan and bring to the boil. Stir the mussels occasionally while they are cooking to help them cook evenly. Cook about 5-8 minutes, or until the shells open. Discard any mussels that do not open.

Spoon the mussels into individual serving bowls and strain the cooking liquid. Pour the liquid into 4 small bowls and serve with the mussels and a bowl of melted butter mixed with lemon juice for each person. Dip the mussels into the broth and the melted butter to eat. Use a mussel shell to scoop out each mussel, or eat with small forks or spoons.

Plaice with Spicy Tomato Sauce

Preparation Time: about 30 minutes **Cooking Time:** 20-25 minutes **Serves:** 4

This piquant fish dish is popular along Mexico's Gulf coast.

Ingredients

90g/3oz cream cheese
1 tsp dried oregano
Pinch cayenne pepper
4 whole fillets of plaice
Lime slices and dill to garnish

Tomato Sauce
1 tbsp oil
1 small onion, chopped
1 stick celery, chopped

1 chilli, seeded and chopped
¼ tsp each ground cumin, coriander
  and ginger
½ red and ½ green pepper, seeded
  and chopped
400g/14oz canned tomatoes
1 tbsp tomato purée
Salt, pepper and a pinch sugar

Heat the oil in a heavy-based pan and cook the onion, celery, chilli and spices for about 5 minutes over very low heat. Add red and green peppers and the remaining sauce ingredients and bring to the boil. Reduce heat and simmer 15-20 minutes, stirring occasionally. Set aside while preparing the fish.

Mix the cream cheese, oregano and cayenne pepper together and set aside. Skin the fillets using a filleting knife. Start at the tail end and hold the knife at a slight angle to the skin. Push the knife along using a sawing motion, with the blade against the skin. Dip fingers in salt to make it easier to hold onto the fish skin. Gradually separate the fish from the skin. Spread the cheese filling on all 4 fillets and roll each up. Secure with cocktail sticks. Place the fillets in a lightly greased baking dish, cover and cook for 10 minutes in a preheated 180°C/350°F/Gas Mark 4 oven.

Pour over the tomato sauce and cook a further 10-15 minutes. Fish is cooked when it feels firm and looks opaque. Garnish with lime slices and dill.

Swordfish with Grapefruit Salad

Preparation Time: about 35 minutes **Cooking Time:** about 8-10 minutes
Serves: 4

Rich and dense in texture, swordfish takes very well to a tart grapefruit accompaniment.

Ingredients

4-6 ruby or pink grapefruit
   (depending on size)
2 limes
1 spring onion, finely chopped
2 tbsps chopped fresh coriander or
   parsley

1 tbsp sugar
2 tbsps oil
Black pepper to taste
4-8 swordfish steaks (depending on
   size)
Coriander sprigs for garnish

Remove the zest from the grapefruit and 1 lime with a zester and set it aside. Squeeze the juice from the limes. Remove all the pith from the grapefruit and segment them. Mix the grapefruit with the citrus zests and the onion, coriander, sugar and half the lime juice and set aside.

Mix remaining lime juice, oil and pepper together and brush both sides of the fish. Place under a pre-heated grill and cook for about 4 minutes each side depending on distance from heat source. To serve, place a coriander sprig on each fish steak and serve with the grapefruit.

Appetisers and Soups:
  Crab and Sweetcorn Soup 12
  Coconut Fried Fish with Chillies 24
  Fish Fried with Garlic Sauce 18
  Fish Tempura 10
  Moules Mariniére 22
  Oysters Rockeffeller 16
  Prawn Soup 20
  Szechuan Fish 14
Baked Stuffed Mackerel 30
Chilled Fish Curry 32
Coconut Fried Fish with Chillies 24
Cod Curry 62
Crab and Sweetcorn Soup 12
Curries:
  Chilled Fish Curry 32
  Cod Curry 62
Dressed Crab Salad 38
Entertaining:
  Fish Milanese 48
  Grilled Herrings with Dill and
    Mustard 52
  Halibut and Crab Hollandaise 60
  Monkfish and Pepper Kebabs with
    Bearnaise Butter Sauce 44
  Mussels in White Wine Sauce 64
  Paella 46
  Sardine and Tomato Gratinée 58
  Spiced Salmon Steaks 56
  Trout with Herbs 26
Fish Milanese 48
Fish Tempura 10
Fisherman's Stew 54
Fried Fish with Garlic Sauce 18
Grilled Herrings with Dill and Mustard 52

Halibut and Crab Hollandaise 60
Monkfish and Pepper Kebabs with
  Bearnaise Butter Sauce 44
Moules Mariniére 22
Mussels in White Wine Sauce 64
Oysters Rockeffeller 16
Paella 46
Pies and Flans:
  Plaice and Mushroom Turnovers 36
  Smoked Haddock and Egg Quiche 42
  Salmon Pies 50
Plaice and Mushroom Turnovers 36
Plaice with Spicy Tomato Sauce 66
Prawn Soup 20
Salads:
  Dressed Crab Salad 38
  Swordfish with Grapefruit Salad 68
Salmon Pies 50
Sardine and Tomato Gratinée 58
Smoked Haddock and Egg Quiche 42
Spiced Salmon Steaks 56
Spicy Baked Prawns 34
Stews:
  Fisherman's Stew 54
  Tomato Fish Stew 28
Stuffed Fish:
  Baked Stuffed Mackerel 30
  Plaice with Spicy Tomato Sauce 66
  Spicy Baked Prawns 34
  Stuffed Sole 40
Stuffed Sole 40
Swordfish with Grapefruit Salad 68
Szechuan Fish 14
Tomato Fish Stew 28
Trout with Herbs 26